Being In Time
With Children

Being In Time With Children

Reflections on the moments between us

David Kuschner

Also by
David Kuschner

The Child's Construction of Knowledge: Piaget for Teaching Children
(with George Forman)
THE NATIONAL ASSOCIATION FOR THE EDUCATION OF YOUNG CHILDREN, 1983

From Children to Red Hatters®: Diverse Images and Issues of Play
(editor)
UNIVERSITY PRESS OF AMERICA, 2009

International Perspectives on Children's Play
(co-editor with Jaipaul Roopnarine, James Johnson, & Michael Patte)
OPEN UNIVERSITY PRESS, 2015

Handbook of the Study of Play (Volumes 1 and 2)
(co-editor with James Johnson, Scott Eberle, & Thomas Henricks)
ROWAN & LITTLEFIELD, 2015

COVER PHOTOS:
COLOR David Kuschner
BLACK & WHITE Lauren Harel

TEXT ILLUSTRATIONS: Samakarov

Copyright © 2019 David Kuschner

Published by
STICKY EARTH BOOKS
Exton, Pennsylvania
StickyEarth.com

Paperback ISBN 978-0-9986449-2-9
Library of Congress Control Number: 2019931848

To Leslie,
my partner on this almost half-century journey.
Thank you for everything.

To Emily,
who grew from the young daughter in these pages to
become the incredible mother of our granddaughter.

And to Lily,
who is showing me once again what it means to
be in time with a child. Hearing the words, "my David"
in your voice is a moment in time that I treasure.

ACKNOWLEDGMENTS

There may be one name on the cover of this book but as they say, it takes a village to raise a book. The village I would like to thank includes -

Annette Murray, of Sticky Earth Books, for shepherding the manuscript from typed pages to its final form as a book. And thanks to Janet Ruth Falon for introducing me to Annette and Sticky Earth Books.

George Forman for first showing me what it meant to marvel at the development of children. The spirit of all those blackboard sessions and film viewing of children's block play has stayed with me all these years.

The late Vito Perrone, my dean at the University of North Dakota, for modeling what it meant to respect the real children behind the theories and curriculum approaches.

The authors and others whose borrowed words support and in some cases inspired my reflections about being in time with children.

Robin Schild, who read an early in-the-file-drawer version of this book and whose kind words helped motivate me to finally take it out of that file drawer.

My friends and colleagues at the University of North Dakota and the University of Cincinnati for sharing the respect for children that I hope is reflected in these pages.

My friends from *The Association for the Study of Play* - Tom Henricks, Michael Patte, Jim Johnson, Marcia Nell, Walter Drew, Fraser Brown, Dorothy Sluss and Alice Meckley - for all the years of inspiring presentations and thought provoking conversations.

My daughter, Emily, for being the original inspiration for the book and for allowing me to share some of our moments together.

My wife, Leslie, for her encouragement, unwavering belief and all the moments that have been and will be.

TABLE OF CONTENTS

the secret of life

I ONCE STOOD IN FRONT OF THE SHELVES labeled "Child Care" in a local bookstore and counted books. I wasn't an employee of the store: personal and professional curiosity brought me to that rather odd moment. I was curious to see just how many books were written with the intent of imparting wisdom and guidance to parents. Since I was interested in the total number of *different* books I was careful not to tally multiple copies of the same title. It took a while for me to finish because every time I thought someone was paying attention to what I was doing, I stopped counting and tried to look interested in a particular book.

There were 103 different titles on those shelves. If a parent actually read all 103 of those books, some of the things she could learn included how to: discipline her child, avoid raising a brat, calm a crying baby, cope with a defiant child, teach her child to be tolerant, talk with her child about sex, deal with whining, sleep problems, and sibling rivalry (not all from the same book, however), teach math, reading, writing and responsibility to her child, (again, not from the same book), build a healthy mind and unlock learning potential, raise an only child, support development of her child's self esteem, and end the homework hassle.

I did notice that there weren't any books about simply being with children.

> *The secret of life is enjoying the passage of time.*
> *Any fool can do it. There ain't nothing to it.*
> JAMES TAYLOR

time runs through our fingers

SOME NATIVE AMERICAN CULTURES BELIEVE in a concept known as ceremonial time. It is a belief that under certain, special circumstances, the past, present, and future can all be felt and experienced in a single moment; for an instant, all that has come before and all that is yet to be, converge into the right here and right now.

There are moments when just standing still looking at a child can evoke something akin to the feeling of ceremonial time. We watch our child at play, or in deep communion with a friend, or peacefully asleep in her bed, and right at that singular moment in time we can be flooded with memories of the living that has brought us to this time and with the imaginings of the future that will emerge from our child's place in the present. Our thinking about the past can let such words as guilt, regret, and pride emerge, and when we think about the future we are likely to find our thoughts expressed in terms of dreams, hopes, worries, and anxieties. But perhaps the Native Americans had it right: it is best to think of these moments as a time to stand still, to pause, to be in the present, and to celebrate.

> Time with children runs through our fingers like water as we lift our hands, try to hold, to capture, to fix moments in a lens, a magic circle of images or words.
> LOUISE ERDRICH

the baby is suddenly gone

MY DAUGHTER (THEN IN HIGH SCHOOL), MY WIFE, AND I were sitting in an airport when we saw a young college student saying goodbye to her parents. She appeared to be boarding an airplane to return to school at the end of a vacation break. As the three of us gazed somewhat shyly upon this tender scene, I noticed the tears welling up in my wife's eyes.

I guess it is true that if you stand very still, sometimes you can see into the future.

The baby is suddenly gone. I never took my eyes from him - it happened while I was watching and I never saw it.

MARC PARENT

the child is a gift of nature

THE FRENCH PHILOSOPHER, JEAN-JACQUES ROUSSEAU, was persecuted, excommunicated, threatened with arrest, and forced into exile in the late 1700s for writing, among other ideas seen as blasphemous, that children were born innately good, that *"Everything is good as it leaves the hands of the Author of things; everything degenerates in the hands of man."* Rousseau wound up in so much trouble because his views ran counter to a prevailing religious belief of the time that children were the inheritors of 'original sin,' and therefore in need of parenting and discipline practices that would 'beat the devil' out of them.

It seems as if, more than 250 years later, we are still trying to figure out which it is.

The child is a gift of nature, but the image of the child is mankind's creation.
DAVID ELKIND

be with what is

WHEN WE SIT QUIETLY WATCHING OUR CHILD, there are so many directions in which we can look. We can look up, into the future, with all the worries of what will become of that child of ours. Or we can look down, to the past, and regret everything we have done that might affect that future. Or we can look straight out, at the child standing in front of us, at our child in the right here and the right now.

> *There are people who begin the zoo at the beginning, called the WAYIN, and walk as quickly as they can past every cage until they get to the one called WAYOUT, but the nicest people go straight to the animal they love most, and stay there.*
> A.A. MILNE

> *Be with what is so that what is to be may become.*
> SØREN KIERKEGAARD

to develop a magnificent human being

IT'S BEEN OVER THIRTY YEARS SINCE I FIRST READ the book and yet I not only remember the words, I remember the page the words are on: 12. In the story about her daughter with autism, Clara Claiborne Park writes the following on that page number twelve.

I knew only that my fourth child was not like the others, who needed me and loved me, as I loved them. The fairies had stolen away the human baby and left one of their own.

I remember wondering what this mother could mean by those words. Clearly, she believed her daughter to be human and that she was speaking in somewhat metaphorical terms. The remainder of that book and the sequel that she published twenty years later, make it quite clear that her daughter with autism, although different, lives firmly on the continuum of humanness. But the question of what it means to be human and what it means to raise a human being have stayed with me ever since I first encountered those words on page twelve.

And since then I found more words that keep asking the same question.

To develop a magnificent human being stirs considerably less admiration than to paint a great picture or expand a successful industry.
LEONTINE YOUNG

It is clearly easier for us to imagine ourselves living among better appliances than among better human beings.
MIHALY CSIKSZENTMIHALYI

the vision of babies

BABIES ARE BORN QUITE NEARSIGHTED. Using tests that track eye movements, researchers are able to determine at what distance the eyes of babies can focus and clearly see objects in their environment. It turns out that for the infant, the world beyond a foot or so away is pretty fuzzy.

But consider what there is to see within that foot, what the newborn *can* see clearly. Think about holding a newborn in your arms. Perhaps it is feeding time or perhaps you are holding her just because you want to. Think about gazing down into her eyes as those eyes stare back up at you. Your face is within that one-foot distance; your face is not fuzzy at all. Your baby can see *you* just fine.

> *Babies seem designed to see the people who love them more clearly than anything else.*
> ALISON GOPNIK, ANDREW MELTZOFF
> & PATRICIA KUHL

parental fictions

THE SCIENTIFIC EXPLANATION: The human baby is born rather helpless and dependent on we adults to provide for her survival. Without us, the stark truth is that a human baby, unlike snake, alligator, or guppy babies, will die. But the human baby isn't really born totally helpless; she is born with certain reflexes that will help her enter the community of persons. Some of these reflexes develop into important skills and abilities and some seem to have no real purpose and disappear as the young infant matures.

One of the important reflexes is the grasping reflex. Put an object into the tiny palm of a baby and those little fingers close around the object. It isn't intentional or thoughtful on the part of the baby; it is an inborn, reflexive response. The object and the pressure it puts on the smooth skin of that tiny palm triggers the reflex. The baby - the hand - can't help but close. Muscles automatically move, pulling bones, cartilage, and skin with them, and grasp whatever it is that triggered the response. Muscles, cartilage, bones, skin, neurons firing, synapses connecting - it's all reflexive, instinctual, beyond the baby's control.

A MOTHER'S EXPLANATION: A mother looks down at her peaceful baby lying in the crib. The mother leans over and smiles, and just wants to touch the new person she has recently brought into the world. She takes her finger and ever so lightly places it in the palm of her baby's hand. The tiny fingers curl tenderly around the mother's, muscles automatically moving, pulling bones, cartilage, and skin with them, grasping whatever triggered the response. The grasping of the mother's finger is not intentional or deliberate, except of course to the mother. She doesn't see muscles, cartilage, and skin; she sees a person, a social being.

"Oh, look," the mother says to no one in particular, "She's holding my hand."

> *In a way, the parents are entertaining a fiction,*
> *but it is a fiction with a function.*
>
> KENNETH KAYE

a child's goal

I WAS ONCE "REPRIMANDED" BY A DAY CARE CENTER DIRECTOR for tying a pair of shoes. The wearer of the shoes, a four-year-old girl at the center, had asked me for help and without giving it much thought, I knelt down and tied the laces of her sneakers. The center director, who had been watching this small moment in time, then approached me and gently suggested that I had deprived the little girl of an opportunity to develop autonomy and independence and that we have to encourage children to do things for themselves so they won't be dependent on adults.

True. Autonomy and independence are good things and we want children to develop in that direction. But, I wanted to say (and didn't because, if truth be told, I was a bit intimated by this woman), there is a difference between being *dependent* and being able to *depend* on people. That little girl needed her shoes tied so she could rejoin her friends in play. She saw me as an adult upon whom she could *depend* to help her get done what she needed to get done. I was happy to be there for her. There would be plenty of other opportunities to practice shoelace tying.

> *A child's goal is not to become a successful adult...*
> *A child's goal is to be a successful child.*
> JUDITH RICH HARRIS

power

DURING ONE OF MY GRADUATE SEMINARS, a student brought in his eighteen-month-old son so I could do some demonstrations related to the cognitive development of toddlers. The boy and I were sitting at a table in the front of the room. I had presented a set of tabletop blocks to him and we were all watching how he was spontaneously manipulating the block pieces and combining them into small groupings. At one point he stacked a couple of blocks on the table and then accidentally knocked two blocks to the floor. He paused a second, and then leaned over a bit and stared at the blocks sitting on the floor. He then sat back up and turned in his chair to look at me. After fixing his gaze on my face, he extended his arm towards the blocks on the floor, pointed one finger at them and clearly, directly, and with great definitiveness said, "Go get!"

What a wonderful magician this child was. Simply by making eye contact, extending a finger, and putting two small words together, this eighteen-month-old was able to levitate an adult right out of his seat, move that adult across the floor, make him bend over, pick up the blocks, and bring them back to the table so that his play could continue.

Eye contact. Finger point. Two words. Power.

> *She was standing at the threshold of an almost inconceivable power, the ability to tell us stories, to hold our attention with words, to create something in her own head and plant it in ours, like feeding us, mouth to mouth.*
>
> **BRIAN HALL**

being in another's presence

THIS IS MY RIGHT HAND...#1

Our daughter was playing in her bedroom with one of her friends from the day care center. I was reading a magazine in the living room when they came rushing over to me, full of excitement. They had figured out why, when facing each other, their right hands were not directly opposite each other but were on different sides of their bodies.

"I'm Jewish and Kelly's not," was my daughter's explanation.

THIS IS MY RIGHT HAND...#2

About a week or so after the incident described above, my daughter found me in the study and again told me that she understands the problem with right and left hands. Facing me, she lifted her right hand, said, "This is my right hand," and after pointing across her body to my right hand, said, "And this is your right hand." She then repeated the process with her left hand. I sat there proudly thinking to myself that our daughter was terrifically bright when, still facing me, she then said:

"And when I get older, this [raising her left hand, the one opposite my right hand] will be my right hand and this [raising her right hand, the one opposite my left hand] will be my left hand."

The illusions of parents are so easily shattered.

> *Being in another person's presence while she*
> *so honestly labors in an astonishingly intimate*
> *activity – the activity of making sense – is*
> *somehow very touching.*
> **ROBERT KEGAN**

it's not always the big things

PICTURES OF BIRTHDAY PARTIES, visits with grandparents, first days of school...they fit in frames, lay flat between album covers, and collect in boxes on shelves in the basement.

The sound of "Hi Daddy" in your tiny voice lives in my heart.

And also - this is almost too much to handle - when I hold him now, he puts an arm around my neck.

ANNE LAMOTT

It's not always the big things that mark a change - not the graduation ceremony or the wedding bells, not the champagne toast or popping balloons and flowing streamers. Sometimes the biggest change is marked by nothing more than the smallest melody that's suddenly forgotten, the favorite set of jeans outgrown, the round cheeks that flatten, the lock of hair that turns blond to brown.

MARC PARENT

it's hard not to be a bother

OUR FRIEND WATCHED HER DAUGHTER and a playmate through the kitchen window. The two four-year-olds were playing in the sandbox in the backyard and as might be expected from two exuberant preschoolers, sand began to leave the sandbox in ways that were unacceptable to the mother. One visit outside was followed by a second with the mother reminding the children to keep the sand in the sandbox. When the offense was committed for a third time, the mother sternly addressed the children and warned them that if they kept throwing the sand out of the sandbox, they wouldn't be allowed to play in the sand anymore that day.

Before our friend could return to the kitchen, her daughter stood up from the sand, walked over to her mother and calmly said: "Mom, why don't you go inside and hide."

To a kid, grownups are not a superior version of us: grownups are them.
JUDITH RICH HARRIS

Sometimes you have to watch it when you're a grown-up. It's hard not to be a bother.
MARC PARENT

out of the mouths of babes

THREE GENERATIONS RIDING IN GRANDPA'S CAR.

Grandpa:	Emily, what does the red light mean?
Emily:	Stop.
Grandpa:	And what does the green light mean?
Emily:	Go.
Grandpa:	And what does the yellow light mean?
Emily:	Cooperation.

Out of the mouths of babes...

OLD TESTAMENT

what's on their minds

AT A GATHERING OF EXTENDED FAMILY, one of the little cousins, maybe four-years-old at the time, was misbehaving a bit. After a few warnings, her mother got up, walked over to her, took her by the hand, and said, "We have to go into the other room and talk."

As they were leaving the room, the little girl turned her head towards the people she was leaving behind and said, "I hate when this happens."

Two of the nice things about young children are that, unlike babies, they can tell you what's on their minds, and, unlike older children, they do.
MELVIN KONNER

actually

ACTUALLY: AS A MATTER OF FACT, IN TRUTH, TRULY; INDEED; EVEN. Not said of the objective reality of the thing asserted, but as to the truthfulness of the assertion and its correspondence with the thing; hence added to vouch for statements which seem surprising, incredible, or exaggerated: 'He has actually sent the letter after all.'

OXFORD ENGLISH DICTIONARY

ACTUALLY: ADVERB:1. In point of fact: indeed, really. *See* REAL, TRUE. 2. At this moment: currently, now. Idioms: even (or just) (or right) now. *See* TIME. 3. In truth: fairly, genuinely, indeed, positively, really, truly, truthfully, verily. Idioms: for fair. *See* REAL, TRUE.

ROGET'S THESAURUS

ACTUALLY: actual (*adj.*), actually (*adv.*), actuality (*n.*) All three have frequent (and often semantically half-empty) use as intensifiers or hyperbolic helpers. *In actual truth* means "In real truth" and underscores the truth of this truth, as contrasted with the untruth of the "truth" you've heard before. *Actually,* like *really,* seems to try to dispel doubts as yet unexpressed. *In actuality* means "Here's what really happened." All three words have useful literal senses too, but care is required to evoke them. See REAL. Compare FACT.

THE COLUMBIA GUIDE TO STANDARD AMERICAN ENGLISH

ACTUALLY: "Actually, I have two trucks."

5-YEAR-OLD BOY

Each of Elly's words started in the public domain. Yet it was as if as soon as she acquired it, it became her own and nobody else's.

CLARA CLAIBORNE PARK

I've always wanted to be normal

AS I ANTICIPATED THE BIRTH OF MY CHILD, I was determined that I would never be the kind of parent who compared his child to other children. I would just accept my child for who he (or she) was and not worry that other children of the same age were talking earlier, walking further, or using the potty-chair sooner.

Our daughter was born at five o'clock on a Friday afternoon. As fate would have it, the maternity ward was very quiet that afternoon. In fact, our daughter was the only baby born that evening and occupied the nursery all by herself. She was a small baby, weighing in at five pounds, fifteen ounces and measuring just under eighteen inches. But as I looked at her through the nursery window or as she lay in her mother's arms, she seemed like just the right size.

Then, beginning Saturday morning and continuing through the weekend, other babies started arriving, one after the other. When I looked through the nursery window on Sunday morning and saw her lying there, one among a number of other just-come-into-the-world babies, I found myself thinking that our little girl was surrounded by the future offensive line of the local high school football team.

So much for not comparing my child to other children.

Cherish forever what makes you unique, 'cuz you're really a yawn if it goes.

BETTE MIDLER

I've always wanted to be normal but lately I've had a strong suspicion that this is it.

J. SKINNER

waiting for the questions

OUR FRIEND HAD NEVER MET this almost two-year-old before. She got down on our living room floor to talk with the emerging toddler and like many friendly adults, wanted to know what to call him.

"What is your name?" she asked.

"Two," was his reply.

The toddler's mother then told our friend that she had asked her son the wrong question.

Children can be really smart if they are only asked the right questions.

> *My whole life is waiting for the questions to which I have prepared answers.*
>
> TOM STOPPARD

with a name like yours

IT WAS GOING TO BE A SURPRISE. During parent-teacher conferences we learned that our daughter loved playing with the felt board at the day care center so my wife decided to make one for her room at home. She spent a number of nights down in the basement cutting and sewing and preparing what we thought would be a most treasured gift. Along with the board itself, she filled a cigar box with cutout letters, numbers, shapes, and an assortment of little figures that could be used by our daughter to tell and retell some of her favorite stories.

Then the big day arrived. We had our daughter go into her room and close her eyes. When she opened them, there in front of her was this large board covered with felt and the cigar box, which she eagerly opened. Her eyes grew wide with excitement as she quickly dumped the contents of the box on the floor and sat down to play with her new gift. We decided to let her enjoy it on her own without our hovering around, so we walked out of her room.

A few minutes later she called to us to come in and see what she had done. As I walked toward her room I had visions of words, arithmetic equations, and detailed stories played out on the board with the felt pieces my wife had created. As I entered the room I was stunned to see not a piece of felt on the board but what I did see, in black magic marker, reaching almost from one side of the board to the other, were the letters,

E M I L Y. (Her name.)

My first reaction was to yell. To scold. "Do you know how long your mother worked on this? Do you know how much this is going to hurt her? Look what you did. You ruined your felt board!"

But I didn't. In the split second between thinking those thoughts and opening my mouth, I realized something else. We had been calling her by that name from the moment of her birth. We helped her learn how to say it and spell it and rejoiced with her once she mastered control of markers and the letters and was able to put her name down in print. Those black marks on the felt covering that board made perfect sense. We had given this gift to her. She was laying claim to it. In the world of words, your name is the only word that doesn't stand for something general, something abstract. It stands for you; it is specific to the person who owns it.

Words and equations and stories eventually did find their way onto that flannel board. They were all put there by E M I L Y.

> *"Don't stand chattering to yourself like that,"*
> *Humpty Dumpty said, looking at her for the first*
> *time, "but tell me your name and your business."*
>
> *"My name is Alice, but –"*
>
> *"It's a stupid name enough!" Humpty Dumpty*
> *interrupted impatiently. "What does it mean?"*
>
> *"Must a name mean something?" Alice asked*
> *doubtfully.*
>
> *"Of course it must," Humpty Dumpty said with*
> *a short laugh: "my name means the shape I am*
> *– and a good handsome shape it is, too. With a*
> *name like yours, you might be any shape, almost."*
> LEWIS CARROLL, THROUGH THE LOOKING GLASS

faith and patience

WE HAVE THE PICTURE TO PROVE IT. At about the age of nine months or so, our daughter, all by herself, lifted a drinking cup up to her mouth and drank some juice. It was one of those wonderful two handled, lidded, with sucking-spout cups that are just right for the emerging drinker. We were amazed at this newfound ability, especially how early it was manifesting itself. Our daughter was precocious. Our daughter was developmentally advanced. Our daughter was special. Clearly this meant our daughter would score in the high 1500s on the college SAT tests and be accepted to an Ivy League school of her choosing. We were convinced that this cup drinking at such an early age probably foreshadowed a Nobel Prize in medicine for discovering a cure for some incurable disease.

After that one glorious moment captured on film, our daughter didn't drink from a cup by herself for about another five months.

Development is funny like that. We would like to think that children develop in a straight line, always moving forward and progressing to greater and greater accomplishments. In general and over the long scope of time this is true, but when looked at on a moment-to-moment and day-to-day basis, it just doesn't work that way. There are fits ands starts and even steps backwards. The child who utters a perfectly intelligible word on Tuesday may revert to nonsensical babbling for two more weeks before that word or others resurface. Their developmental timeline is just that, theirs.

Our children's task is to keep moving forward. Our task is to be patient.

Faith, then, is the inner dimension of patience.
STEPHEN NACHMANOVITCH

playing with letters

MLE.
The first way in which our daughter spelled her name.

MLE for Emily.
Concise. To the point. Makes perfect sense.

FVBT.
First word other than her name that our daughter wrote.

FVBT for 'EVERYBODY.'

'EFF...VEE...BUH...TEE'
Also makes sense. She knew the names of the letters
of the alphabet – how many times had she heard the
alphabet song? – and when she wanted to spell a word
she found the sounds she needed in the letter names.

Eventually our daughter learned to spell her name
as it appears on her birth certificate and she learned
how to spell words like 'everybody' as they appear in the
dictionary.

Her spellings may be more correct now but I'm not
sure they are nearly as interesting.

*John and I were encouraged by the fact that Katie,
who was now only a month shy of two years old,
seemed fairly interested in playing with letters.
She had already learned to spell 'Mom,' 'Dad,' and
her own name. True, she had also flushed several
of the letters down the toilet, but we felt these
were acceptable losses in our quest to raise a
literate toddler.*
MARTHA BECK

a self

SITTING ACROSS THE AISLE FROM US on the train, he spent the two-hour journey wriggling, squirming, and exploring like most toddlers would do. Pacifier in mouth, he spent some of the time on his parent's lap, wrestling with his older brother, or visiting with his grandmother sitting one row further up. His eyes never shut during the two hours, the pacifier came out of his mouth only when a cookie went in, and he never spoke a word.

About an hour into the trip, he made a discovery. If he stood up on the seat and turned around, his eyes would be at about the same height as a 1x3 inch shiny, metal plate that was affixed to the wall behind him. I watched as he looked at the plate for a bit. Then the game began. First, he would hold on to the back of the seat bench and crouch down as if he were hiding from the metal plate. Then, with great joy, he would pull himself back up to look at the plate again. He did this four or five times, squealing with delight each time he pulled himself up to be eye level with that small, shiny plate.

As I watched him, I tried to figure out what was bringing him so much joy. When I looked closely at the metal plate, I realized what he was doing. He could see his reflection in the plate and he was playing peek-a-boo with himself. When he crouched down, he was gone, and when he stood back up, he was there again. While it is true that he never spoke a word during the two-hour train ride, during these few minutes of crouching, standing, and grinning, it seemed to be clear what he was at least saying to himself: HERE I AM!

> *A self is probably the most impressive work of art we ever produce, surely the most intricate.*
>
> JEROME BRUNER

living in space, not in time

EACH MORNING, I WOULD WATCH our daughter and her friend as they began their journey to school. And each morning one of the main differences between children and adults would be made perfectly clear. Here they were, dawdling down the driveway, talking with each other, sometimes arguing with each other, and here I was, beginning to become anxious about their getting to school on time. They would dance, walk backwards, look at some squirrels madly dashing across some lawn, be distracted by a pebble on the street. I would stand in the doorway muttering under my breath, "C'mon, girls, get going, you are going to be late for school." Of course they would continue to dawdle, walk much too slowly for my comfort, talk some more, dance some more, and be together some more. They walked to school together, leaving from our house or the friend's house, for most of third grade through sixth grade. They were never late for school.

Perhaps it comes down to a difference in what we see. I, the adult, saw the hands of the clock moving closer and closer to a particular number and I, the adult, saw only a beginning and end point to their journey. They, the children, saw the squirrels, the pebbles, the opportunity to talk, argue, dance, walk backwards, and experience everything in-between.

*The child...knows neither the past nor future,
sees, knows, becomes the present more than
we can understand or remember. For him space
and temporality are limitless, and each distinct
experience, whether or not he has had it before,
adds another chapter to an unending sequence
of newness.*

ROBERT GRUDIN

*For as long as I can recall, I have lived in space,
not in time.*

OSKAR KOKOSCHKA

know how to listen

FOR SIX YEARS I directed the honors program at the university. Part of my job was to talk with high school seniors (and sometimes their parents) about the honors program and what we had to offer. During these conversations I would often ask questions of the student, trying to get a sense of interests, learning style, educational goals, etc. One time I was talking with an eighteen-year-old young woman and I asked her about the types of environments in which she learned best. Did she like hands-on courses, lectures, discussions? If she came to the university, what kind of teaching style would be the best fit for her? In what kind of course would she be most successful? In which of her high school classes did she do the best? How would she describe herself as a learner?

"I had a natural talent for being quiet," was her answer.

The language of truth can often be heard in silence, if we only know how to listen.
ROBERT LAWRENCE SMITH

beckoning objects

A TINY PIECE OF PAPER ON THE FLOOR. Electrical outlets. Pots and pans in the kitchen drawer. The corner of the rug in the living room. Your favorite CD in your precious CD collection. The wires that carry the sound from your favorite CD. The books on the bottom shelf of the bookcase in the study. The book covers on the books on the bottom shelf of the bookcase in the study. The leftover food in the dog's dish. The twig carried in on the bottom of a shoe. The shoelace in the shoe. The pen you left on the table next to the sofa. The pad of paper with the shopping list you jotted down with that pen. The penny (or nickel or dime or quarter) that dropped out of your pants. Lint from a belly button. The television guide from the newspaper. The squiggle that is part of the pattern in the kitchen linoleum. A pea from dinner two nights ago. The receipt that you couldn't find when you were balancing the checkbook. A thread just barely loose in the sleeve of a sweater. The almost-not-there crack in the tray of the highchair. The television remote control. The hinge on the kitchen cabinet. The doorstopper behind the bathroom door. The toilet paper in the bathroom. Almost anything.

> *In so doing, she manifested a rather typical age-pattern of exploratory behavior, where things...have many unlimited possibilities to be experimented with and acted upon in a world of "beckoning objects."*
>
> **VALERIE POLAKOW SURANSKY**

stuff

ONE OF THE BEST PRESENTS my wife and I ever gave
our daughter was a cigar box full of stuff. She was
about four years of age and her absolutely favorite kind
of play activity was to pretend. One day she might be
a teacher, the next day a waitress, and then maybe a
storekeeper. She could occupy herself for hours in her
room just pretending.

The cigar box was filled with the stuff any self-
respecting teacher or waitress or storekeeper would
need. We visited the local office supply store and
bought markers, tape, receipt pads, a roll of tickets (if
you are going to put on a show with your students you
need tickets for the audience), 4x6 cards (great for
making menus), stickers, play money, and all sorts of
other stuff. When we gave her the cigar box, you would
have thought we had given a teenager the keys to her
new car.

Sometimes what children need is the stuff they
need.

*Stuff: 1. The material out of which something
is made or formed; substance. 2. The essential
substance or elements; essence.*
**THE AMERICAN HERITAGE DICTIONARY
OF THE ENGLISH LANGUAGE, FOURTH EDITION**

*We are such stuff
As dreams are made on...*
WILLIAM SHAKESPEARE

one must ask children

I ONLY SAW A PILE of round Oriental rugs and since we weren't in the market for round, they held no interest. But for this little girl there was, as the saying goes, more there than meets the eye.

When she came upon the stack of rugs, she knew what they were. Without much hesitation, she climbed onto the top of the pile, which put her about two and a half feet from the floor of the store. She quickly laid face down, spread her arms and began to move her arms and feet in an outward, swirling motion.

"Butter melting on pancakes," she explained to her mother.

> One must ask children and birds how cherries and strawberries taste.
>
> JOHANN WOLFGANG VON GOETHE

> Kids: they dance before they learn there is anything that isn't music.
>
> WILLIAM STAFFORD

explore and experiment

A SCENE PLAYED OUT COUNTLESS TIMES WITH COUNTLESS VARIATIONS. Your child is sitting in a highchair with you seated right in front of her. It is meal time and all of the tools of the trade are arranged within easy reach: jars of baby food, samples of appropriate finger food, plastic dishes, slightly damp face cloths, and spoons.

This can be a happy time; your child is enjoying her food and you are enjoying this pleasurable time with your baby. And then the inevitable happens. You watch as she grasps and picks up a spoon - Ah, you think, she is going to make an attempt to feed herself - but it is not to be. She grasps the spoon, lifts and moves her arm so the spoon is being held over the edge of the highchair, and then drops the spoon. The spoon makes a slight pinging noise on the floor and she leans over to look at its landing spot.

You are in a good mood so you bend down from the chair, pick up the spoon from the floor before the dog gets to it, wipe it off with the damp cloth, and place it back down on the highchair tray. All the while the eyes of your child are watching you very intently. Of course, the whole process repeats itself. She grasps the spoon, lifts, reaches, drops, and looks. And this time, she now looks at you and smiles. You are still in a good mood so you bend down, retrieve the spoon, wipe it off again and replace it back on the highchair tray. You have faith that all of this may just be a prelude to your child using the spoon for its designed and intended purpose, to transport food into her mouth.

Now she's got you. Not much hesitation anymore. The spoon is grasped, lifted, directed, and released. And now the smile has turned into a giggle. Not quite angry but not quite in the same good mood, you once more retrieve the spoon, place it with some authority on the highchair tray and say somewhat firmly, "Spoons are not for dropping."

Remember those "Look Who's Talking Movies," where we heard the voiceover of the cute baby expressing all of those droll and clever comments? Well, if your baby in the highchair could talk, this is what she might say about your definitive statement that 'spoons are not for dropping.'

"Mother, I have to disagree with you. That's exactly what they are for at this exact moment in time. You see, I only recently discovered that I could pick things up and drop them so I like to practice. There is just something about doing what I know how to do that is fun. Oh, eventually I get bored with it but at the beginning it is fun to keep practicing. And I have also discovered that when you are practicing, things happen that you don't know were going to happen. Like when I dropped the spoon I didn't know it would make a noise. I liked that so I wanted to see if I could make the noise happen again and maybe I could make a louder noise if I threw the spoon down harder. New stuff is fun. And you know what I was going to do next time, before you stopped me with your mean face and your hand on my wrist? I was going to reach out so when I dropped the spoon it would land over there on the carpet. I wanted to see if the sound would be different. But you wouldn't let me. And you know what else is fun? Watching you bend over to pick up the spoon from the floor. I like playing with you."

> *We are born with the ability to discover the secrets of the universe and our own minds, and with the drive to explore and experiment until we do.*
> **ALISON GOPNIK, ANDREW N. MELTZOFF,**
> **& PATRICIA K. KUHL**

create and destroy

ON A SATURDAY NIGHT, more than forty years ago, I learned why young children get great pleasure from building up block structures and then gleefully knocking them over into great piles of rubble.

A friend of mine had recently divorced and was about to remarry. Not wanting any vestiges of his former relationship and on the verge of receiving a whole new set of wedding gifts, he (and his wife-to-be) wanted to dispose of an old set of china dishes. Throwing them away or giving them away would have been too easy. The solution reached that Saturday night: destroy them with a BB rifle.

Taking turns, we each lay prone in the living room, took aim down the hallway into the kitchen, and over a couple of hours, methodically shattered cups, saucers, serving bowls, creamers, and dishes of various sizes.

It was fun.

Create and destroy, create and destroy, a power beyond anything else in her experience.
BRIAN HALL

let's play doctor

WEDNESDAY, APRIL 3, 2002

I read in the newspaper today that British doctors were able to use gene therapy to cure a little boy who was born without an immune system. Without an immune system, this 18-month-old was always in danger of serious infections and as a result had to spend his life in a completely sterile environment, not able to interact with other children. He was, as we have come to call these children, a "Bubble Boy."

In the gene therapy procedure the doctors removed some of the boy's bone marrow, added a 'good' copy of the defective gene to his bone marrow, and then re-injected the bone marrow back into his body.

The procedure was a success and the toddler's mother said that the treatment has changed her son's life significantly: "We see him now playing with other children and it is just amazing."

Who could have imagined?

WEDNESDAY, APRIL 3, 2002, SOMEWHERE

Preschooler to a playmate: "Let's play doctor. I'll be the doctor and you'll be the one who is sick."

> *A lot of parents ask me...whether children who daydream, have imaginary playmates, and play make-believe games are in danger of becoming emotionally disturbed. I tell them that the main danger they're in is the danger of becoming a highly successful scientist or artist, because the research shows that these people engaged in a lot of play, including pretend play, when they were children.*
> **BRIAN SUTTON-SMITH**

nature surely did not

A STORY SHARED BY A GRADUATE STUDENT. The student's four-year-old son had an ear infection that required the taking of an antibiotic. The doctor and the boy's parents might have thought that the medicine was a good idea but they certainly hadn't consulted the boy about it; he wanted no part of this solution to the ear infection. The parents decided that there was no choice and began to try every possible method of getting him to swallow the supposedly good tasting liquid. They tried to reason with him and although he might have understood the reason, the power of that reason did not sway him. They attempted to bribe him with the promise of special treats but apparently the treats just weren't special enough because he still wouldn't budge from his determination not to cooperate with the treatment for his illness. Finally, his parents decided they would resort to taking away his favorite toy. His father took the toy and put it up on a high shelf, too high for the child to reach by himself...even if he pulled a chair over. The parents made it quite clear - with the most serious tone they could muster - that he would not be able to play with the toy until he took his medicine.

Faced with these circumstances, the boy simply replied, "That's ok. You can't take away my ideas and put them on the shelf."

And then he went about his playing.

> *Nature surely did not design children to be putty in their parents' hands.*
> **JUDITH RICH HARRIS**

the final piece of love

LETTING GO OF THE BICYCLE SEAT just when she finds her balance.

Letting go of her hands in the pool just when she finds her courage.

Pausing in the story reading just when she has figured out the word for herself.

Quieting our voice just when she has found her own.

Retreating to the shadows just when she has found the spotlight.

It's hard to say how we know when is the right time, but sometimes we just know.

This is the final piece of love. It's just as everyone has said. It's not complete until you let it go. Love grows bigger as you loosen your grip, because only as it floats away do you begin to see what it really is.

MARC PARENT

grownups never understand

CONVERSATION WITH
NINTENDO PLAYING DAUGHTER

Father:"Emily, pay attention to the screen.
You're talking with me and not watching
what you are doing. Your little Mario man
keeps dying."

Emily: "Dad, you and Mom are just alike.
It's only a game."

*Grownups never understand anything by
themselves and it is tiresome for children to be
always and forever explaining things to them.*

ANTOINE DE SAINT-EXUPÉRY

another chance to play

AT SOME POINT IN TIME, the scientists who study the human body figured out breathing. They figured out the process by which the lungs take in air, extract oxygen, move that oxygen into the bloodstream, work with the heart to circulate the oxygenated blood around the body, and bring that blood back to the lungs so that the carbon dioxide waste product can be removed and excreted. The scientists who figured all of this out knew that the process was vital and necessary to the functioning and very existence of the human being.

But once this process was figured out, the scientists didn't then go back to the subjects who do the breathing (the human beings) and try to convince them of the importance of breathing. They didn't try to convince them *to breathe* because breathing is vital and necessary. You don't have to convince a human being to breathe and you don't have to teach them how to breathe. They just do it. The scientists discovered the 'how' of something the human being already knew how to do and something the human being just does. Breathing is simply a part of being human and being alive.

So is the play of children.

We got a small blackboard and we had so much fun running and chasing each other. I was trying to play so much. I told my mother later I was playing as much as I could because I had the feeling that if something happened and fighting and shelling came back, I may die and I will never get another chance to play.
10-YEAR-OLD GIRL IN LEBANON

secret of happiness

ONE OF MY MEMORIES OF CHILDHOOD and living in the house of my parents was my father's reaction to lights left on. He would yell from wherever he found what in his mind was the wanton waste of electricity and make it known that he was not pleased. When I became a parent, I decided that my relationship with my daughter was not going to revolve around kilowatt-hours.

We can choose to go to battle with our children over lights left on, messy rooms, unkempt hair, unfinished glasses of milk, dogs not fed, missing remote controls, clothes left on the floor, pianos not practiced, or no hat on a winter's day.

Or not.

> *The secret of happiness lies not in events but in our responses to them.*
> BARRY NEIL KAUFMAN

the mother strokes, the father pokes

BEING A FATHER, LESSON #1

We heard her cry from the other room. This was her typical pattern. She wasn't one of those babies who woke up and occupied herself in the crib for a half hour or so. Not our daughter. When she was up she wanted someone to come and get her at that very moment. I stirred first and decided that I would go get her and bring her into our bed so perhaps we could get a few more minutes sleep. I slipped out from underneath the covers - noting that neither my wife nor the dog sleeping on the chair next to the bed seemed to be aware that anyone in the house was awake - and headed towards the baby's room.

I was sleepy – our daughter wasn't yet sleeping through the night so a full night's sleep was just a warm memory from the past - but I tried to muster up the energy and good cheer with which to greet our daughter. I entered her room, walked over to the side of the crib and with a big, sweet smile, said, "Hi kiddo."

She was standing in the crib, holding onto the railing with two hands. When she realized who had come in to rescue her from the crib, she let go one of her hands, pointed a finger at me, and said, quite emphatically if I remember correctly, "No!"

I turned around, walked back to our bedroom, slipped under the covers next to my wife, and said, "Honey, she wants you."

BEING A FATHER, LESSON #2

The house we moved to right around our daughter's first birthday was basically a ranch, with the kitchen, dining room, and living room up towards the front of the house and then a long hallway that led to the study, two bedrooms and a bathroom. I think this long hallway contributed to our daughter learning to walk fairly early because shortly after we moved in she became quite an accomplished toddler, using that hallway for practice.

One day, all three of us were standing in that hallway, for a reason I cannot now remember. Our daughter was down at the end by the bedrooms, I was in the middle having just come out of the study, and my wife was standing towards the end of the hallway that connected to the living room. I do not remember what brought us to that moment or what our daughter was doing when she was walking down the hallway and fell. She really hadn't hurt herself but did scare herself enough to start crying. Once she got herself back up onto her feet, she started running down the hallway towards us. (Remember, I was standing in the middle of the hallway and my wife was some number of steps beyond me at the end of the hallway.) I crouched down and spread my arms so that she could get a hug and be comforted. I was still in that position when she went right past me to her mother some fifteen feet behind. That was where the comforting would come from that day.

Mothers and fathers are both important in a child's life. Mothers and fathers do, however, occupy different spaces in the life of their child and sometimes a mother's arms may just be softer.

> We didn't know it at the time, but we were filling stereotypical complementary roles, since mothers tend to soothe their babies and fathers tend to stimulate them. The mother strokes, the father pokes. The mother hymns, the father rhymes.
>
> BRIAN HALL

one of those human blind spots

THERE ARE TIMES when we have to be satisfied if we simply get our child to do what we would like her to do. She may not do it with a smile, she may not do it in good humor, and she may be angry with us as she is doing it. She may pout, sulk, and act and look annoyed. She doesn't want to clean up her room, she resents us for making her clean up her room, and she is not happy that she has to be cleaning up her room when she would much rather be talking on the phone with her best friend. We may want her to say...

"Oh Dad, I have seen the errors of my ways. You are so right. I should assume my fair share of the chores around the house and be responsible for my things. I apologize for being selfish. You are so wonderfully wise!"

...but what we get is that pouty, sulking, unbelievably annoying look on her face. What *we* want to say at that moment is something like...

"You know, everyone has to chip in around here. I am tired of picking up after you. And I'm tired of having to fight you on this every time I ask you to do something around here. You know how much we do for you? Is it too much to ask for you to help out sometimes?"

We'd be better off if we just left the room. She is picking up her clothes and toys. That may be enough of a victory for today.

> Grown-ups are always and forever falling into
> the ancient trap that children must somehow
> incorporate adult emotions and desires in their small
> bodies or else have none at all. It is one of those
> human blind spots that costs everyone dear.
> LEONTINE YOUNG

good little children

AN IMAGINED CONVERSATION

Parent to a three-year-old:
Will you please stop doing that! You know you can be so immature sometimes.

Three-year-old to parent:
Well what do you expect? I'm three.

Immature: Adjective: 1. Not fully grown or developed. See synonyms at young.
THE AMERICAN HERITAGE DICTIONARY
OF THE ENGLISH LANGUAGE: FOURTH EDITION, 2000

We want our kids to behave like good little children, and good little children don't behave like grownups.
JUDITH RICHMAN HARRIS

you're a crank

OVERHEARD IN A DEPARTMENT STORE (AS RETOLD BY MY WIFE AND DAUGHTER) The mother and her two young boys had apparently been in the store for a little while, perhaps doing some back-to-school shopping. At this moment, the boys were tussling over who would be the one to push the shopping cart. As they were engaged in some brotherly pushing and shoving, their mother stopped and just stood there while she said:

"Could we please go down one aisle without any embarrassment?"

> *I use my most soothing tone of voice to call her names. The tone helps her, the words help me...*
>
> *You're a crank! I whisper, holding her tenderly. A goddamn crank! You're driving me completely nuts!*
>
> **LOUISE ERDRICH**

life is not a problem that can be solved

SOMETIMES OUR CHILDREN *can*, but *won't...*
and that may be the time to ask, "Why?"

Sometimes our children *can*, but *don't know how...*
and that may be the time to ask,
"How may I help you?"

And sometimes our children simply *can't...*
and that may be the time to be silent and wait.

> *Life is not a problem that can be solved. It must*
> *be lived each day, and each day brings a jumble of*
> *choices that challenge our practical wisdom, our*
> *common sense, and our yearning for truth.*
> ROBERT LAWRENCE SMITH

learning from bees

OVER THE YEARS I HAVE FOUND wise words about being with children in some rather odd places. Ever since learning about the keeping of bees from Sue Hubbell, for example, I have thought that some of her perceptions applied to being with children as well as to being with bees. Here are the guidelines she followed to keep the bees from being "cross."

> I am seldom stung...because I don't often do things that make them cross...I long ago gave up a number of beekeeping practices conceived with the notion of making the bees do certain things that seemed good from a human development standpoint but which usually involved radically disrupting the hive...I watch the bees more, try to understand what they are doing and then see if I can work in a way that will be in keeping with their biology and behavior. I try to create conditions that will make them happy, and then leave them alone as much as possible.

Try to avoid doing things that make them cross. Understand them from the perspective of their lives. Watch closely. Be with them in a way that is matched to who they are. Try to keep them happy. Give them space and time. Get stung less often.

Sounds like reasonable parenting advice to me.

minor irritants

THE PROCESS BEGINS when a tiny piece of sand or some other minute particle makes its way inside the oyster shell. Because this tiny piece of sand is irritating and annoying, it triggers the secretion of substances from within the oyster and these substances begin to coat the piece of sand, layer by layer. Over a period of time, the piece of sand, the tiny, little irritant, is entirely encapsulated by the substance secreted by the oyster. Now it is no longer a tiny piece of sand; no longer an irritant. It is a pearl.

Something to keep in mind when our children are annoying and irritating.

> *In the end, it's not what we keep our children from that will save them. It is what we put into them in the first place.*
>
> MARC PARENT

not good news

MATURING. Growing up. Developmental progress.
These are all words that suggest wonderful times ahead.
But with every step forward comes new problems.
Our backs didn't hurt as much *before* our new toddler
learned how to climb the stairs. Our ears were less
offended *before* our preschooler decided to borrow
some of the words used by his new friends. Our sleep
was less fitful *before* our teenager learned how to drive.
I guess we know our children are developing nicely
when our backs hurt, our ears are offended, and we
aren't sleeping very well.

> *Sam can climb the stairs now.*
> *I don't think this is good news.*
> **ANNE LAMOTT**

trying not to laugh

IT HAPPENS TO MOST PARENTS at some point in time. Your child does something that by most standards of behavior is wrong, mischievous, inappropriate, or an example of being 'bad.' Under normal circumstances, your child would be scolded or punished for what he or she did. But there comes a time when the 'bad' behavior is so funny that you find yourself smiling instead of scolding, laughing instead of punishing.

"Come look," our daughter calls to us from the bathroom. We look. "I'm giving Raggedy Ann a bath," she says. We see.

It took Raggedy Ann a while to dry out from her bath in the toilet.

> She made it into a running gag, Madeleine's
> pasta-on-the-head routine, whereby she slew
> us night after night. I've mentioned power,
> and to make people laugh is a heady draft
> of it, since laughter is not only spectacular
> but involuntary. Not wanting to encourage
> her to play with food, I tried not to laugh,
> and Madeleine could tell I was trying, and
> time after time – at the sight of her big head
> completely filling the circle of her arms, her
> dainty fingers affixing the piece of pasta
> to its top like a well-licked postage stamp,
> "Hat? Hat?" – I failed, turning my face away,
> snorting, unmanned.
>
> BRIAN HALL

human nature is contagious

I HAD VISITED THE DAY CARE CENTER ON CAMPUS to videotape the children during their free playtime. As I had done in the past, I was going to show the tape to the children. They enjoyed watching themselves on the television screen and it provided an opportunity for the teachers to comment on some of the interesting things that had taken place during the activity time. On this particular occasion, I was having trouble getting the videotape to play. I connected the cables between the video machine and the television monitor, but all that appeared on the screen was 'snow.' Getting a bit nervous – there were, after all, sixty-four children and about ten teachers sitting and standing behind me – I started to fiddle with the cables and the controls trying to figure out why I wasn't able to get a clear picture. The room became quiet as minutes-feeling-like-hours passed as I worked on the machines. Then, out of the quiet behind me, came the voice of George, one of the more lively children in the center.

"That fuckin' channel. That fuckin' channel."

George was also one of the more verbal children in the center.

> Since for better or worse human nature is
> contagious, the children are pretty apt to catch it.
> **LEONTINE YOUNG**

the possibility of untruth

THERE IS A THIN LINE between lying and being
a storyteller, between fibbing and pretending,
between not telling the truth and considering all the
possibilities, and between a little child fabricating a
story and Steven Spielberg filming "E.T." We may not
like it when our children lie and tell fibs, but the ability
to do so springs from the deep well of what makes us
human: the power to imagine alternative realities, to
lift ourselves out of the here and now, and express our
dreams through words.

We may not like it when our children lie, but
imagine what it would be like if they couldn't.

*The possibility of untruth is the price we pay for
the general flexibility of language.*

EDMUND BLAIR BOLLES

*She can't lie. That's almost true. Ten years ago it
was true. Today, now and then, she manages the
transparent lie of a three-year-old caught with his
hand in the cookie jar; she's come that far. I'm not
the only parent of an autistic child to count it as
progress. Real lying, however, controlled, effective
insincerity, is forever beyond her compass...
The inability to lie convincingly could pass as a
diagnostic indicator of autism.*

CLARA CLAIBORNE PARK

what do you do?

WE THOUGHT WE HAD PREPARED HER. It was the first Halloween that she would be old enough to participate in and we had many discussions as to what was going to happen. Candy would be in the bowl on the tray table not far from the front door. When the doorbell rang, you pick up the bowl, carry it to the door, open the door, see how many children are there and give each of them two pieces of candy. It seemed as if we discussed and rehearsed this procedure endlessly. Candy by door. Doorbell rings. Count the children. Two pieces for each child. For the couple of weeks leading up to October 31, nothing brought more excitement than the anticipation of the ringing doorbell.

And finally, Halloween arrived. The first ring of the doorbell, she runs excitedly to the candy bowl, takes it in her arms, and goes to answer the door. We thought we had prepared her so well. We thought we had gone over the procedure clearly and thoroughly. But somehow we forgot to tell her that children would be in costumes and some of these costumes might be scary.

First ring of the doorbell. She opens the door and there it was: scary. The bowl of candy goes flying in the air and the little girl, so excited about her first Halloween, goes flying down the hallway to her room.

We thought we had prepared her so well.

How do you say to your child in the night,
"Nothing's all black, but then nothing's all white"?
How do you say, "It will all be all right."
When you know that it mightn't be true?
What do you do?
STEPHEN SONDHEIM

the truth is

EVENTUALLY, AND INEVITABLY, our children will encounter something bad, maybe even something horrible. A gash on the head from a collision with the coffee table. A slight from a supposed best friend. The death of a beloved pet or a grandfather. It will happen. Life has a habit of getting in the way of itself every now and then. The simple fact is that we parents will, at some point in time and probably more than once, fail in our role as protectors and shielders of our children. But we won't stop trying.

> *The truth is that I can no longer explain most things, nor can I make them any better with words.*
>
> BETH KEPHART

renegotiated balances

BEING A PARENT means learning how to be comfortable with ambiguities, gray areas, tension, dilemmas, conflicts that can't be resolved, situations when there are two sides to every story, more than one valid opinion, no easy solutions, no definitive answers, a sense of being in limbo, and a problem that just won't seem to go away. We will find ourselves uttering the words, 'and, but, maybe, perhaps, either, or', sometimes all in the same sentence. This can be that, always can be sometimes, and permanent can quickly become temporary (and vice versa).

Borrowing from the words of the educator Peter Elbow, our lives as parents will be full of 'contraries' and perhaps we should just 'embrace' them.

> But could we be parents in the full bloom of
> who we are – open, honest, strong, vulnerable,
> sometimes clear and sometimes confused?
> **BARRY NEIL KAUFMAN**

> I suggest that human development involves a
> succession of renegotiated balances.
> **ROBERT KEGAN**

a holy land

THERE YOU WERE, pushing your long-handled broom, trying to sweep clean the black asphalt of the driveway. And there she was, your little girl in her gingham dress, pushing her just-the-right-size broom behind you.

It is true: Love can be painted even on the canvas of a grass-strewn driveway.

> The only difference between a place to live and a holy land is the number of footsteps you've put into the ground.
>
> MARC PARENT

enjoying being a parent

THE PARENTS STOOD on either side of the bookrack, trying to grab some time to browse through the latest bestsellers. Their young daughter, who had her legs but not much language, was doing her own browsing, finding the specks of paper on the floor to be as exciting as the newest Grisham or Clancy thrillers were for the grownups. The girl's mother was slightly more anxious about the daughter's whereabouts than the father and was regularly checking to make sure that *he* knew exactly where their daughter was and what she was into. He kept reassuring her that, yes, the little girl was in his sight, and yes, she was fine.

But all this watching for the daughter was keeping the father from his browsing so now when his little girl came to touch base with him, he greeted her warmly and in a most pleasant tone, said, "Where's Mommy? Go find Mommy." It was clear from the expression on her face that the little girl liked this game and she quickly toddled around the bookrack and found her mother's leg to grab onto, all with a giggle that suggested a treasure was located. (And it was clear from the expression on the father's face that he knew what game he had just begun.) The mother, who was also trying to do her own browsing, heard her husband's chuckle and understood what was going on and after greeting her daughter equally warmly, returned the volley and said, "Where's Daddy? Go find Daddy" and off the little girl went.

There were smiles all around.

> *Parents are meant to enjoy parenting. If you are not enjoying it, maybe you're working too hard.*
> JUDITH RICH HARRIS

you don't even have to try

HOLIDAY SEASON and I learned a new song today. I learned it from the father standing behind me on the escalator at the mall. He was singing the song as he held one son in his arms and held the hand of the other son standing by his side. The song went something like this:

"We are going up the escalator, going up the escalator, going up the escalator today."

Before Amanda was born, I never heard Susan talk baby-type talk, even in jest. Now it is second nature. She isn't at all self-conscious about it. And I must confess - in the middle of those long nights I have sung a chorus or two of "Rockabye Baby in the Treetop" myself. There's no humorous intent. When you're holding your baby, those sorts of things come out of your mouth. You don't even have to try.

BOB GREENE

to be present

THE BOY AND HIS MOTHER sat down across the aisle from me. We had a few minutes before the plane was scheduled to depart and the boy quickly discovered the drop-down tray on the seatback in front of him. He began to entertain himself while his mother took care of getting their bags settled.

We were delayed somewhat in taking off but for the boy the delay meant only more time playing with the tray. Up and down it went, sometimes going back up with great force. I felt sorry for the person who was in the seat on the other side of the tray but she displayed great patience and tolerance for his activity. I am not sure I would have been as forgiving.

But I felt more sorry for the mother when the flight attendant made the announcement that we were preparing for take-off and that ALL TRAY TABLES MUST BE RETURNED TO THEIR LOCKED AND UPRIGHT POSITIONS. I didn't think that her son would respond very favorably to this directive and I was right. As soon as his mother wrestled the tray table out of his grip, the fussing and squirming began.

Of course there was delay between the time of the announcement and the plane actually getting into the air. We were not first in line for take-off and that lengthened the time before he would be able to play again with the tray. His mother did the best she could to divert his attention and find something else with which he could play.

Finally, a book pulled out from the bag under the seat seemed to catch his interest and he settled down a bit in his mother's lap. She began reading the story to him and this was the magic elixir to soothe his spirit. He leaned back into her chest, helped her turn the pages, and together they read.

While their joint attention to the book was taking place, the woman sitting next to the mother, perhaps out of sympathy, began talking to her. The mother, perhaps out of politeness or out of a desire to converse with an adult, accepted the entrée for conversation. What happened at that point was fascinating to watch. Every time his mother would turn her attention away from the book and to an exchange of words with the woman, the boy would start fussing and squirming in her lap again and somewhat violently kicking the seat in front of him. For minutes this wordless 'dialogue' between mother and son went on: pay attention to the book and to me and I am quiet and attentive; pay attention to the woman and I am not happy.

I sat across the aisle from that young boy for approximately two and a half hours and I never heard him utter a word. I don't know if he possessed any language; I only know that during the flight from Ohio to Florida, he didn't use any. But with his fussing and his squirming and his kicking he appeared to be communicating to his mother quite clearly.

BE with me.

Be WITH me.

Be with ME.

To be present but unresponsive often communicates a failure to value. To say, as we all do at times, 'That's nice,' or 'Very good,' or 'Good for you,' is such a meager way to evidence interest.

FRANCES POCKMAN HAWKINS

asking for the world

BOOKSTORE, COLUMBUS, OHIO

I watched as the young boy – he looked to be about three years of age – walked up to his father, his arms wrapped around a box so large that his arms could not completely encircle it. Inside the box was a globe of the world.

"Daddy, can I have this?" was the question he asked his father.

If only it were that easy.

Every child asks for the world, every parent can give it to them. It's just that the world they ask for has nothing to do with anything that can be bought.

MARC PARENT

Madeleine reached for the moon in her first months and then appealed to us, hoping we might hand it to her. Of all her quaint infant illusions, this struck the deepest chord in me, some old echo of my own childhood. In the silver light out in the yard, I felt sorry for both of us that I could not bring the moon close. We say that love on a face shines, and the shine of the moon still feels like a certain kind of love to me, a love that in the quiet of the night, in the unprying light, seems patient and tolerant. In other words, a parental love.

BRIAN HALL

opening the door

I WATCHED THEM IN THE RESTAURANT. Lovely family. Two children, one a toddler in a highchair. At one point a waiter came over and tied a balloon to the back of the highchair. A toy was created. The balloon occupied the young child's attention and this allowed the parents and the older sibling to attend to their food with fewer distractions.

Helium filled, the balloon floated some with the air currents moving through the restaurant. At one point the string of the balloon moved beyond the toddler's reach. She tried but her extended arm just didn't extend far enough. Noticing her desire and intentions, her mother, almost absent-mindedly, reached out and retrieved the balloon but didn't bring the string all the way back into the waiting grasp of her daughter. She moved the string towards her daughter's hand and within her reach but she waited for her to make that effort; the parent did her part but now the child had to do hers.

"I will bring the balloon back to you," the mother's actions said, "but you must extend your arm and reach for it."

"I will bring the world close to you," the mother's actions say. "Reach. Grasp."

Teachers open the door,
but you must enter by yourself.
ANCIENT CHINESE PROVERB

our humanity

A NOT UNUSUAL SCENE, #1

Sally is engrossed in populating her block castle with people and animals when she hears her preschool teacher say that they have five more minutes to play before group time begins. She also hears the excitement in the teacher's voice as she informs the children that, "We will be learning some new and fun songs this morning during group time!"

Sally continues placing the little figures in and around the castle that she had spent considerable time constructing. The two towers had been particularly troublesome because the blocks just didn't want to stay balanced but Sally had solved the problem by rearranging the blocks so the bigger pieces were on bottom and by placing the towers against the outer walls for support. She felt pretty proud of her solution. Getting windows into the towers also proved to be a problem and Sally solved that one by deciding that towers didn't need windows.

Sally really didn't have much of an idea how long 'five minutes' was but she knew time was passing until she would be expected to leave her castle and join the rest of classmates for singing, something she really didn't like doing. She felt nervous about not knowing the words to the songs and she didn't like how Peter's voice seemed to always be louder than everyone else's. Sally moved around to the other side of the castle. Maybe her teacher wouldn't see her over there.

How ever long five minutes were, they did pass and Sally did hear her teacher say that play time was over and that they had to put the materials away and that they had to join everyone on the carpet and that they would be starting group time and that they would be learning new songs.

When Mrs. Russell, the teacher who announced the group time, did a quick check of who was and who wasn't sitting on their bottoms on the carpet, she quickly realized that Sally wasn't there – again. She knew the two places to look. First she checked the block area. There she saw a rather complex block structure with walls and towers and people and animals but no Sally. Then she checked the book table over by the window and as she expected, there was Sally, sitting under the table, leaning back against the wall, hands clasping her knees.

"Mrs. Peters," said Mrs. Russell to her assistant teacher, "would you please get the children started on the songs. I'll go get Sally. How many times has it been this week?"

A NOT UNUSUAL SCENE, #2

You are at a Saturday evening cocktail party. There are about twenty or so people there and even though you had some initial anxiety about coming, the evening is turning out to be quite pleasant. You know some of the people but many you are meeting for the first time and you have found some of the conversation to be stimulating and interesting. There is soft music playing in the background and the food that is strategically placed around the rooms is plentiful and quite good.

About an hour and a half into the evening you find yourself engrossed in a friendly political discussion with a couple of other guests. You are impressed with the knowledge they possess but you also feel pretty good about how well you are expressing your own opinions. You are in the middle of making a point when you hear the hostess call for everyone to gather in the living room. As soon as everyone is there, she makes the following announcement: "There is still more food to come and time for more conversation but now is the time for us to play charades. I have a list of the teams and..."

You don't really hear the end of what she has to say because all you can think of is how much you hate playing charades. You are not very good at it, you don't like being the center of attention, you don't like performing in front of people, and you don't like being laughed at even when it is good natured and all in good fun. That's what charades means to you and you are quickly trying to figure out how you can avoid participating in the game. Maybe if you quietly move to the back of the group you won't be noticed and you can just fade into the crowd. But the hostess said that she has made up teams. That means she has a list of names and yours is on one of the lists. Maybe you can just argue that you are terrible at the game and it would be a disservice to the others for you to be a member of anyone's team, and that you can be a judge or scorekeeper or maybe can start washing dishes in kitchen. Or maybe you will look at your watch, feign surprise at how late it is and remember some reason why you must be leaving: a child at home, an early morning appointment, a cat to let out. Something. Anything.

Children are most like us in their feelings and least like us in their thoughts.

DAVID ELKIND

Our humanity is most evident in our feelings.

DANIEL GOLEMAN

the rhythm of a child

SCENE #1 (REAL)

I am holding my daughter's hand as we walk down the elementary school hallway to visit her mother.

It is after the schoolchildren have left, so the only people still around are teachers in their classrooms, making the transition from a day just ended to the one that will begin the next morning. As we walk down that hallway, teachers who recognize me and know of our daughter from my wife's stories, call out to us and because children are more interesting than the parents, use her name in greeting: "Hi Emily," rings out from one doorway after another.

With each greeting, Emily moves closer and closer into my body until she is almost glued to my legs. Seeing this, one voice from within a room follows up her "Hi, Emily," with, "Oh, she's so shy."

SCENE #2 (IMAGINARY)

You are walking down a street in some foreign city you have never before visited. You know no one there except the traveling companion by your side. As you walk down the street taking in the sights, strangers begin to greet you by name. First one, then another, then another. You can't walk ten feet without someone cheerfully saying hello to you, but not an anonymous hello from a friendly stranger; no, these people know your name. There may be smiles on their faces and their greetings may be pleasant, but you are not comforted. Who are these people and how do they know my name?

> ...by the time we've reached adulthood, it's not what we've learned that makes us who we are, it's what we've forgotten. Moving to the rhythm of a child is a dance of remembrance...
>
> MARC PARENT

and I have another choice

I ONCE SERVED as the leader of a 'Fathers-Only' discussion group. Twelve men, all with children at the same preschool program, came together once every two weeks to discuss issues related to being a father. The discussions were interesting, sometimes spirited, and frequently poignant.

During one of the sessions, I posed the following question to the fathers, asking for a show of hands before we entered into a discussion about the question itself.

"When you think about how you are as a father with your child, are you trying to be just like your own father, or are you trying to be the opposite; do you find yourself trying to be like the father you feel you never had?"

There was no hesitation on anyone's part. Each of us in that room knew the kind of father we wanted to be.

The final tally was evenly split.

And I have another choice – to accept what I didn't get to choose. I could have wished for a calmer nature and on and on, a very long list, but what I finally get to choose is that tiny space between all the givens.

In that tiny space is freedom.

SUE BENDER

we can change

IT WAS A MILDLY FUNNY TELEVISION SHOW based on a fairly ridiculous premise. The mother of a young girl dies and the girl goes to live with the two men who could possibly be her father. The two men were cut from the *Odd Couple* mode, one a somewhat immature playboy type and the other, a hyper-responsible, uptight type. As I said, it was mildly funny.

There is a scene from one episode that has stuck in my memory, however. The uptight, maybe father is lecturing the young girl about some behavioral transgression when he stops in mid-sentence and notices the finger that he has been pointing and shaking at her. It is his comment that I remember.

"When did I get my father's finger?"

> *We can change. We can be different. We can defy history...Our past is but a memory dragged into the present moment...And in the next moment, we can change it all.*
>
> BARRY NEIL KAUFMAN

time to be the grown-up

ONE NIGHT, in the house on North 25th street, I awoke in the middle of the darkness and made my way down the long hallway to the living room. Our baby daughter was asleep in her crib and her mother was asleep in the bed that I had just left. I stood in the living room, engulfed in the silence, when the strangest feeling came over me. I stood there, alone in the dark, thinking that there was supposed to be a father someplace in this house.

> *It's a jarring moment in life when*
> *it's time for you to be the Grown-up.*
> JON KATZ

careful the things you say

DIBS IN SEARCH OF SELF is the story of a young boy's year in play therapy. During one of their weekly sessions, the therapist informs Dibs that the furnace in the building isn't working and that some men are trying to fix it. Dibs asks, "What is wrong with it?" and the therapist replies, "I don't know." And then Dibs says...

"You could find out, you know..."

"I could? How?"

"You could go down in the basement and hang around out of the way on the edge of things close enough to watch them and hear what they have to say..."

"I expect I could..."

"Then why didn't you?"

"To tell you the truth, Dibs...It had not occurred to me to do that."

"You can learn lots of interesting things that way..."

Careful the things you say.
Children will listen.
Careful the things you do,
children will see and learn.

STEPHEN SONDHEIM

looking for strengths

THERE IS A CURIOUS PARADOX in our lives as parents. It is sometimes so easy for us to find reasons to scold, correct, and to say 'no.' Yet when our children present us with moments of kindness, warmth, and grace – and they do - we can be so silent.

Looking for strengths is an act of love.
HERBERT KOHL

if you know I can do it

REST ASSURED, there *will* come a time when our children won't do something we want them to do. (OK, there will be many times they won't do what we want them to do.) They may not want to pick up their toys, finish their macaroni and cheese, change into their pajamas, review for the arithmetic test one more time, or swallow the cough medicine. When faced with all of their "I won't" or "I don't want to," again rest assured, that some version of the following words will come out of our mouths: "I know you can do it" (i.e., I know you can pick up your toys, finish your food, put on your pajamas, study some more for the test, and take your medicine). We will probably utter those words as sweetly as we can and with a smile on our face.

Have you ever thought what might be going through the minds of our children when they hear, "I know you can do it"?

"If you know I can do it, then why do I have to do it?"

> *There. My room was clean. Now finally I could play, which meant that all the stuff would come right back out. This business of cleaning your room made no sense but I was starting to be a big kid, seven years old, and while being older of course was fun in many ways, it also entailed additional obligatory goodness.*
>
> PAUL KARASIK AND JUDY KARASIK

what would I feel like if?

MOTHER SPEAKING ON CELL PHONE WITH
DAUGHTER (OVERHEARD IN A BOOKSTORE):
"Now Jennifer, if Mommy and Daddy leave the
bookstore to come and pick you up, you won't be able to
go to anymore sleepovers."

Standing not five feet from the mother, a sense of
sadness came over me as I imagined how lonely and
frightened that little girl must have been feeling at that
very moment.

I also wondered how often we parents say something
we really don't mean.

> *Good parents have no magic key to dealing with*
> *children beyond this almost foolishly simple one:*
> *to try to imagine each situation from the child's*
> *point of view. Some people do it by instinct, but*
> *it is a technique that one can learn - to turn in*
> *upon oneself at need and ask, "What would I feel*
> *like if?"*
>
> CLARA CLAIBORNE PARK

gone forever

IT WAS OUR DAUGHTER'S first 'return-to-home' vacation during her freshman year in college. We were all talking in the kitchen when she bent down and pulled open the bottom drawer to the right of the sink. Where she expected to find the bags of chips, cookies and other snacks that filled that drawer all through her living-at-home-growing-up-years, she found assorted sizes of Tupperware containers with matching lids. Empty Tupperware containers. Upon inquiring, she then learned that the snacks hadn't been moved from their customary location in that bottom drawer to some other cabinet or drawer; they had been replaced by Tupperware.

For some reason, she seemed to think this was symbolic.

She wasn't pleased.

Detailed, synchronous adult conversations exist only in memory. But when I miss these things most, I try to remember that they will all return one day, and the children who've tipped them over will be gone forever.

MARC PARENT

small acts of grace

OVERHEARD IN AN AIRPORT RESTAURANT
    The daughter leaned into her father's body while on the other side of the table, the son snuggled into the mother's. Everyone looked a bit tired from wherever their travels had and would be taking them.
    Father (softly) to daughter: "Look at your mother over there. Isn't she beautiful?"

> *We are thrown together on a temporary planet,*
> *and the only thing we have to protect ourselves*
> *from the fury of our fate is kindness incarnate,*
> *small acts of grace.*
>
> BETH KEPHART

letting go while holding tight

A GAME PLAYED WITH SOME VARIATIONS.

I lie on the floor in the living room and she walks slowly around me. I am humming or singing a song, or perhaps just stringing words together to create some tension. It doesn't matter what I am saying because all she is interested in is that at some point, maybe after ten seconds, maybe after a minute, I am going to reach out and grab her, tumble her down to my body, play at holding her while she plays at fighting to escape, laugh and giggle with her, and then after just the right amount of time, let her go.

"Daddy, let's do it again," she says.

Someone once wrote or said - I am sorry I cannot remember who - that a mother spends a lifetime trying to create distance between a daughter and herself while a father spends a lifetime trying to bridge the distance between his daughter and himself.

My daughter taught me the number one, most important rule of the 'lying on the living room floor' game very quickly: I was not allowed to hold on to her for very long.

> This is our human problem, one common to parents, sons, daughters, too - how to let go while holding tight, how to simultaneously cherish the closeness and intricacy of the bond while at the same time letting out the raveling string, the red yarn that ties our hearts.
>
> LOUISE ERDRICH

respect

I WAS BROWSING IN A LOCAL BOOKSTORE on a chilly winter's day. All of a sudden, through the open door, a toddler rockets into the store. It seemed clear that he had been in this store before because he was comfortable moving about the aisles and it didn't take him long to locate the children's book section. But he wasn't there to settle down in one section or with one book. He was there to see it all and to exercise this newly discovered talent of walking. His mother and father, respectful of his desire to explore (and probably their own desire to browse), stayed a reasonable distance from him but stayed within striking distance. As he moved, they moved, almost in a choreographed fashion, one parent in front and one parent behind. Still, when you are a toddler and you are becoming full of your emerging desire for and ability at autonomy, there are limits to the limits you will accept. This was quite clearly expressed when he stopped in his tracks, turned to face his father who was trailing behind, and exclaimed,

"Stop following me!"

A bridge must be well anchored on both sides, with as much respect for where it begins as for where it ends.

ROBERT KEGAN

the dance

I WATCHED AS THEY WAITED in line with the rest of us, this mother and her young son, he who so obviously had recently discovered the joys of walking.

Like the synchronized swimmers in the Olympics or the prima ballerina and her always-attentive partner, they moved as a team, mother and son, one the explorer and one the watcher. Never more than six feet away, the mother moved as if there were an invisible tether between them. If he moved a few feet, she followed, letting the tether keep them connected. "I respect your need for freedom," the mother's tether said, "but I must also make sure you are safe."

Then, when the young explorer did move too far in the wrong direction, too close to the road, the mother quickly closed the distance between them not only by taking a few steps towards him but also with her words.

"Honey, don't go near the street."

This boy probably didn't know the real meaning of these words but he did feel their touch on his shoulder. He stopped and turned around. His mother smiled at him and took a few steps backwards, away from the direction of the road, and he followed, the invisible tether gently urging him towards safer ground.

> At the heart of all meaningful human relationships, there is only the great dance of life.
> EVELYN B. THOMAN & SUE BROWDER

> A good relationship has a pattern like a dance...the joy of such a pattern is not only the joy of creating or the joy of participating; it is also the joy of living in the moment.
> ANNE MORROW LINDBERGH

letting love grow

I SOMETIMES SEE THEM when I am out for my morning walk. Mothers and children standing on street corners, waiting for the school bus. (I have seen only one father on my usual two-mile route.) I can't help but think what a brave act this is for the two of them: one going and one letting go. I also notice the mother who doesn't turn and leave right away as the bus pulls off down the street. She stands and stares for a few seconds as if her watching will place a blanket of safety around her young child. How hard it is sometimes to be brave.

> *Casey has been in school for the past four months, and the days are different. We opened the door to let him out and world came rushing in.*
>
> MARC PARENT

> *How do you let love grow*
> *You've got to it give a chance when you've found it*
> *A bird in your hand will stay until*
> *You start to close your fingers around it*
>
> DAVID ROTH

it's not fair

TO BE A PARENT is to learn how to wait patiently. First, we wait for the nine months to pass so we can get on with the business of being a parent. Then we begin to wait for all of those developments, those milestones, that tell us our child is growing up. We wait and wait for the first steps and when they come the date and place is noted in the baby journal. Grandparents are called with the exciting news and perhaps the video camera is hauled out to record the monumental occasion for posterity; if we are really technologically savvy, we might film the event and store it on our own website.

Then we wait and wait for the first words to be uttered. Again the date and this time the word is noted in the baby journal and the grandparents are called with the exciting news and maybe even the baby is brought to the phone to repeat his or her brilliance for them.

But all too soon, nature plays its dirty little trick on us. What do we parents get for all our waiting and anticipation? A child who walks away and talks back.

We spend the first twelve months of our children's lives teaching them to walk and talk and the next twelve telling them to sit down and shut up.

PHYLLIS DILLER

free from our stares

DURING HER JUNIOR YEAR IN HIGH SCHOOL, our daughter entered a local arts competition. High school students could compete in a number of categories and she chose voice. She prepared two songs, won a preliminary competition and became one of four students to compete in the finals. It was very exciting.

Naturally she had to practice for the final competition and she did so, accompanying herself on the piano in our living room. One day, as the final competition date rapidly approached, she stood by the piano and spent about ten minutes running through her two songs. I listened from the kitchen and when she finished, something like the following exchange occurred.

Father: *"Emily, that was quick. Shouldn't you practice more?"*

Daughter: *"No, that was enough."*

Father: *"But the finals are only a week away. You need to practice more."* (Imagine an annoyed, parental tone.)

Daughter: *"That is all I am going to do now. I know what I am doing."*

It was at that moment that it hit me. She may or may not have known what she was doing. She may or may not have known what was the best way to prepare for the competition, but one thing was for sure: I didn't. I had never taken voice lessons like she had been taking for the past year. I had never sung in high school musicals or in four performances a week for nine weeks in a summer dinner theater production of "Annie." In reality, I knew virtually nothing about singing, rehearsing songs, saving your voice, warming up your voice, or training your voice. I couldn't carry a tune, let alone prepare for a voice competition. If there were better ways for her to rehearse her songs and get ready for the competition, just because I carried the title of 'parent' didn't mean I was the one who knew what those better ways were.

Yet sometimes we have to learn how to turn our backs on our children, free them of our stares and our judgments, and let them go about their own explorations and experiments.

HERBERT KOHL

the more things change

SOME THINGS NEVER CHANGE, EXAMPLE #1
Circa 1980-1

We tried everything. We would sit by her crib and read her stories in the soft light. Once we thought she was asleep, we would tiptoe out of her room. (We even tried crawling out of the room on all fours.) We tried to stay resolved and let her cry herself to sleep. We consulted with the pediatrician. We spent many nights walking her around the living room. (My wife got into the habit of stacking records on the record player in anticipation of those middle-of-the-night, living room strolls.) Nothing we did seemed to work. Our daughter didn't go to sleep very easily; she just seemed to prefer being awake. She gave up her naps much sooner than her parents preferred and unlike other children we kept hearing about, she rarely fell asleep on the sofa watching television or in the corner of her room in a heap of exhaustion. She just liked being up. (This pattern continued when she attended the day care center. In two years there she actually fell asleep during naptime a grand total of two times – once because her visiting grandfather fell asleep on the cot next to her.)

Circa 1998-2002

Father on phone with college daughter: *"What do you mean you're going out at 11 this evening? Don't you have class in the morning?"*

Father to mother of college daughter: *"Did you see when she sent that email last night? Two-thirty in the morning! What was she doing up at two-thirty in the morning?"*

SOME THINGS NEVER CHANGE, EXAMPLE #2
Circa 1980-81

When our daughter was a baby, nursing was a bit of a challenge. She didn't experience colic or allergies (at least to our knowledge) but nursing wasn't always the romantic, pleasant event about which parents dream. Sometimes nursing brought about fits of fussing, fidgeting, and even crying. Often our daughter didn't nurse for as long as we thought she needed to. At times we were worried that she wasn't getting enough nutrition which led to feelings of guilt, which led to feelings that maybe we weren't very good parents.

Circa 2002

Father and daughter visit a sandwich shop for dinner. Daughter orders a vegetarian sandwich, custom-made: lettuce, pickles, and onions.

Father: *"Emily, you need to have some protein in your sandwich!"*

Emily: *"I'm fine, Dad."*

> *Time does not change us. It just unfolds us.*
> MAX FRISCH

> *Isn't life a series of images that change as they repeat themselves?*
> ANDY WARHOL

> *The more things change, the more they remain the same.*
> ALPHONSE KARR

the energy it takes

IT'S HARD BEING NORMAL, FALL, 1985

Our daughter has started kindergarten and I am on sabbatical from my faculty position at the university. She loves school and is doing well both 'academically' and socially. The reports from her teacher are quite positive, names of friends are beginning to be mentioned, and perhaps most importantly, she wants to go to school each morning.

While she is at school in the morning, I work on my sabbatical projects and then I am home each day to make her lunch and spend the afternoon with her. That may have been *my* plan, however, because after lunch all she wants to do is sit in front of the television (with favorite blanket in hand) and watch Mr. Rogers and Sesame Street. No matter how much cajoling I try, she cannot be persuaded to engage in what at least I think are more productive pursuits. So Mr. Rogers and Sesame Street it is.

One day I watched her sitting in that loveseat staring at the television and a realization came over me. No matter how much she loved kindergarten, no matter how much success both academically and socially she was experiencing during the two and a half hours in that classroom, it wasn't necessarily easy for her. Looking at her holding her blanket I realized that a great deal of energy is expended navigating your way through the school day: figuring out what the teacher wants, conforming your behavior to school expectations, and negotiating relationships with other children. You might be good at it but that doesn't mean there isn't stress involved and that it doesn't wear you out. What I saw on that loveseat was a little girl who had worked very hard succeeding in kindergarten. Doing well and having fun was tiring.

IT'S HARD BEING NORMAL, SPRING, 2002

Our daughter is on the verge of graduating from college. By any criteria she has had a wonderful and successful four years both academically and socially. She developed a great group of friends, was involved in a variety of activities at the college, and has just accepted admission to a very good graduate program at a well-regarded university.

In a recent discussion about what she was going to do this summer before starting graduate school, she made the comment that what she would really like to do is sit in front of the television and 'veg out.'

I wonder if that blanket is still around.

> *One must respect other people's concessions, and recognize that they may have cost more than may appear.*
>
> CLARA CLAIBORNE PARK

> *Nobody realizes that some people expend tremendous energy merely to be normal.*
>
> ALBERT CAMUS

the love of stories

A CHILD…

Cries in her crib when we try to leave the room. Is very upset when we leave her with the babysitter. Will go to a friend's birthday party at McDonalds only if a parent stays. Either refuses to spend the night at a birthday party sleepover or if decides that she will stay, then calls and asks to be picked up to go home. Clings to a leg when we try to say goodbye at the day care center in the morning.

SAME CHILD…

Spends three summers at a sleepover camp (nine hours away from home). Goes to college (thirteen hours away from home). Does a ten-week summer internship in New York City (thirteen hours from home). Goes to London for four months to study (eight hour plane ride from home). Does a ten-week summer internship in Pittsburgh (five hours from home). Goes to graduate school (ten hours away from home).

Sometimes we think that every moment predicts and determines the next. Sometimes it's not that way at all.

> *The Jewish mystics say that God makes human beings because God loves stories…Even God, the mystics are saying, does not know how we are going to come out, so why should we wish for greater control or need it? Better perhaps for us to emulate this kind of God, whose pleasure in us comes not from our obedience to God's laws and regularities, however subject we may be to them, but from God's sheer fascination with how we will live.*
> ROBERT KEGAN

the privilege

AN UNDERGRADUATE STUDENT once approached me after a class session and asked what I remember thinking was a somewhat odd question.

"Do you realize what you said about your daughter during class today?"

Noting the quizzical look on my face and my lack of response, she asked the question a second time.

"Do you remember what you said about your daughter in class today?"

"No," was all I could say because I truly didn't know what she was referring to.

"You said that it was a *privilege* being your daughter's father."

The truth is I wasn't aware that I had uttered those words; they just rose to the surface in the course of the class discussion. But when I heard those words repeated back to me, I was proud to claim ownership.

I still am.

And it still is.

Your children are not your children.
They are the sons and daughters of Life's longing for itself.
They come through you but not from you.
And though they are with you yet they belong not to you.
You may give them your love but not your thoughts,
For they have their own thoughts.
You may house their bodies but not their souls,
For their souls dwell in the house of tomorrow,
  which you cannot visit, not even in your dreams.
You may strive to be like them, but seek not to make
  them like you.
For life goes not backward nor tarries with yesterday.
                                        KAHLIL GIBRAN

if I could save time in a bottle

A PARENT'S VOCABULARY OF TIME...

I'll be right there

In a minute

Just a sec

Hurry up

In a moment

Not now

Maybe tomorrow

I'm waiting

Soon

We're almost there

When I'm ready

When you're ready

When you're older

Sometimes

All the time

Once upon a time

When you were a little girl.

If I could save time in a bottle.
The first thing that I'd like to do
Is to save every day
Till Eternity passes away.
Just to spend them with you.
JIM CROCE

the choices we make

IF YOU WANT your dreams to come true, you must live them while you are awake.

> It is essential to remember that every time we invest attention in an idea, a written word, a spectacle; every time we purchase a product; every time we act on a belief; the texture of the future is changed, even in microscopic ways. The world in which our children and their children will live is built, minute by minute, through the choices we endorse with our psychic energy.
>
> MIHALY CSIKSZENTMIHALYI

the moments between us

MAYBE IT REALLY comes down to moments. This one. The next one. And the one after that. We must be careful with the moments.

He that would do good to another must do it in Minute Particulars.
WILLIAM BLAKE

We do not remember days; we remember moments.
CESARE PARESO

I am done with great things and big plans, great institutions and big successes. I am for those tiny, invisible loving human forces that work from individual to individual, creeping through the crannies of the world like so many rootlets, or like the capillary oozing water, yet which, if given time, will rend the hardest monuments of human pride.
WILLIAM JAMES

The present contains all that there is. It is holy ground.
ALFRED NORTH WHITEHEAD

Each moment is a place you've never been.
MARK STRAND

*At this moment
Present, distant
Shining bubble
Touch it, lose it
Happy, laughing,
Perfect, golden,
Gone.*

JOHN BUCCHINO

SOURCES

The secret of life is enjoying the passage of time... ....*1*
This is the first line of the song, "The Secret O' Life" written and
recorded by singer-songwriter, James Taylor. Recordings of the
song can be found on a number of his albums. There are also lovely
versions of the song recorded by Rosemary Clooney, Nancy Lamott,
and Andrea Marcovicci.

Time with children runs through our fingers *2*
Louise Erdrich, *The Blue Jay's Dance: A Birth Year*, HarperPerennial,
1996, p. 4.

The baby is suddenly gone *3*
Marc Parent, *Believing It All: Lessons I Learned From My Children*,
Little, Brown and Company, 2001, p. 169.

Everything is good as it leaves the hands of the Author of things *4*
This is the first sentence of Rousseau's book, *Emile*. There have been
a number of translations of this book and each translates this first
sentence slightly differently. I have used the translation by Allan
Bloom (Basic Books, 1979, p. 37).

The child is a gift of nature *4*
David Elkind. *Miseducation: Preschoolers At Risk*, Alfred A. Knopf,
1987, p. 52

There are people who begin the zoo at the beginning. *5*
A. A. Milne, *Winnie-The-Pooh*, Dell Publishing, 1954, p. ix.

Be with what is so that what is to be may become *5*
Richard Bode attributes this statement to the philosopher Søren
Kierkegaard in his book, *First You Have to Row a Little Boat:
Reflections on Life & Living* (Warner Books, 1993, p. 191). When I first
read this book, I tried to find the original source for this quotation
and was unable to do so. I wrote the author and he admitted that he
didn't have the original source either; someone had given him the
quotation without a reference citation.

I knew only that my fourth child *6*
Clara Claiborne Park, *The Siege: The First Eight Years of an Autistic
Child*, Atlantic Monthly Press, 1982, p. 12.

To develop a magnificent human being *6*
Leontine Young, *Life Among the Giants: A Child's Eye View of the
Grown-Up World*, McGraw-Hill, 1966, p. 5.

For as long as I can recall *27*
I believe this statement is drawn from the autobiography of the
painter, Oskar Kokoschka. I found it in Vera John-Steiner's book,
Notebooks of the Mind: Explorations of Thinking, Harper & Row, 1985,
p. 21.

The language of truth *28*
Robert Lawrence Smith, *A Quaker Book of Wisdom: Life Lessons
in Simplicity, Service, and Common Sense*, William Morrow and
Company, 1998, p. 29.

In so doing, she manifested *29*
Valerie Suransky, *The Erosion of Childhood*, The University of Chicago
Press, 1982, p. 89.

We are such stuff *30*
William Shakespeare, *The Tempest*, Act IV, Scene 1.

One must ask the children *31*
The quotation from Johann Wolfgang von Goethe appears in Richard
Kehl's, *Silver Departures: Quotations To Set the Mind Traveling*, The
Green Tiger Press, 1983, p. 3.

Kids: they dance before they learn *31*
The quotation from William Stafford appears in Kehl's, *Silver
Departures: Quotations To Set the Mind Traveling*, The Green Tiger
Press, 1983, p. 28.

We are born with the ability *34*
Alison Gopnik, Andrew N. Meltzoff, and Patricia K. Kuhl, *The
Scientist in the Crib: Minds, Brains, and How Children Learn*, William
Morrow and Company, 1999, p. 3.

Create and destroy, create and destroy *35*
Brian Hall, *Madeleine's World: A Child's Journey From Birth to Age
Three*, Houghton Mifflin Company, 1997, p. 20.

A lot of parents ask me *36*
Brian Sutton-Smith is quoted by Paul Chance in his book,
Learning Through Play, Gardner Press, 1979, p. 30.

Nature surely did not design children *37*
Judith Rich Harris, *The Nurture Assumption: Why Children Turn
Out the Way They Do: Parents Matter Less Than You Think and Peers
Matter More*, The Free Press, 1998, p. xiii.

Sam can climb the stairs now *50*
Anne Lamott, *Operating Instructions: A Journal of My Son's First Year*,
Pantheon Books, 1993, p. 213.

She made it into a running gag *51*
Brian Hall, *Madeleine's World: A Child's Journey From Birth to Age
Three*, Houghton Mifflin Company, 1997, p. 108.

Since for better or worse *52*
Leontine Young, *Life Among the Giants: A Child's Eye View of the
Grown-Up World*, McGraw-Hill, 1966, p. 10.

The possibility of untruth *53*
Edmund Blair Bolles, *So Much To Say: How to Help Your Child Learn
to Talk*, St. Martin's Press, 1982, p. 115.

She can't lie. That's almost true *53*
Clara Claiborne Park, *Exiting Nirvana: A Daughter's Life With Autism*,
Little, Brown and Company, 2001, p. 57.

How do you say to your child in the night *54*
This is a lyric from the song, "Children Will Listen," which is from the
musical, *Into The Woods*, lyrics and music by Stephen Sondheim.

The truth is that I can no longer explain *55*
Beth Kephart, *A Slant of Sun: One Child's Courage*, William Morrow,
1998, p. 244.

But could we as parents *56*
Barry Neil Kaufman, *Happiness is a Choice*, Fawcett Columbine, 1991,
p. 191.

I suggest that human development *56*
Robert Kegan, *The Evolving Self: Problem and Process in Human
Development*, Harvard University Press, 1982, p. 81.

The concept of *embracing contraries* is borrowed from Peter Elbow's,
Embracing Contraries: Explorations in Learning and Teaching, Oxford
University Press, 1986.

The only difference between a place to live *57*
Marc Parent, *Believing It All: Lessons I Learned From My Children*,
Little, Brown and Company, 2001, p. 8.

It's a jarring moment. *72*
Jon Katz, *Running to the Mountain: A Journey of Faith and Change*,
Villard, 1999, p. 199.

Careful the things you say, Children will listen *73*
This is a lyric from the song, "Children Will Listen," which is from the
musical, *Into The Woods*, lyrics and music by Stephen Sondheim.

Virginia Axline's book, *Dibs in Search of Self* (Ballantine Books, 1964)
is a true story of a young boy's year in play therapy.

Looking for strengths *74*
Herbert Kohl, *Growing With Your Children*, Little, Brown and
Company, 1978, p. 120.

There. My room was clean *75*
Paul Karasik and Judy Karasik, *The Ride Together: A Brother and
Sister's Memoir of Autism in the Family*, Washington Square Press,
2003, pp. 29-30.

Good parents have no magic key *76*
Clara Claiborne Park, *The Siege: The First Eight Years of an Autistic
Child*, Atlantic Monthly Press, 1982, p. 192.

Detailed, synchronous adult conversations exist only in memory *77*
Marc Parent, *Believing It All: Lessons I Learned From My Children*,
Little, Brown and Company, 2001, p. 173.

We are thrown together *78*
Beth Kephart, *A Slant of Sun: One Child's Courage*, William Morrow,
1998, p. 232.

This is our human problem *79*
Louise Erdrich, *The Blue Jay's Dance: A Birth Year*, HarperPerennial,
1996, p. 69.

A bridge must be well anchored on both sides *80*
Robert Kegan, *In Over Our Heads: The Mental Demands of Modern
Life*, Harvard University Press, 1994, p. 62.

At the heart of all meaningful relationships *81*
Evelyn Thoman and Sue Browder, *Born Dancing: How Intuitive
Parents Understand Their Baby's Unspoken Language and Natural
Rhythms*, Harper & Row, 1987, p. 204.

A good relationship has a pattern like a dance *81*
Anne Morrow Lindbergh, *Gift of the Sea*, Pantheon Books, 1983, p. 104.

LAUREN HAREL

After beginning his academic career at the University of North Dakota, David Kuschner retired as an associate professor emeritus of early childhood education at the University of Cincinnati. He is the co-author of *The Child's Construction of Knowledge: Piaget for Teaching Children*, and an editor of three collections of readings on the topic of play. He was the co-creator and co-host of a weekly radio show entitled, *Considering Children*, for which he conducted interviews with the likes of Dr. Benjamin Spock, Bob Keeshan (Captain Kangaroo), and Alex Haley, author of *Roots*. In 2014 he was the recipient of the Brian Sutton-Smith Play Scholar Award from *The Association for the Study of Play*. He lives with his wife, Leslie, in Philadelphia, Pennsylvania and can be contacted at BeingInTime2019@gmail.com.

Made in the USA
Middletown, DE
12 June 2019